Hidden Worlds
Looking Through a Scientist's Microscope

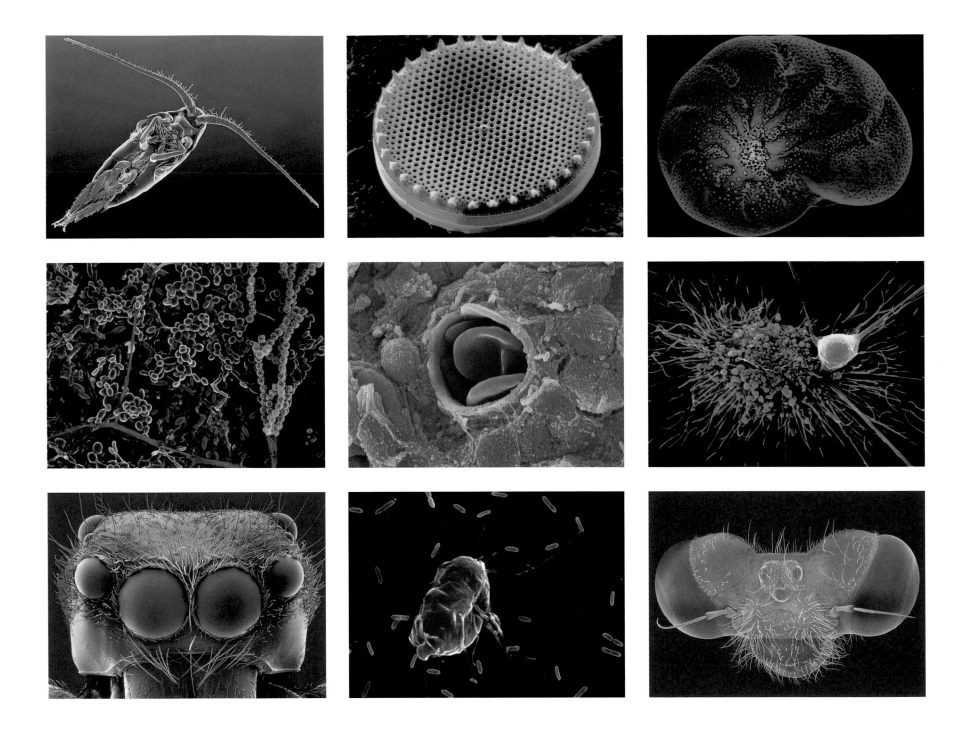

Hidden Worlds
Looking Through a Scientist's Microscope

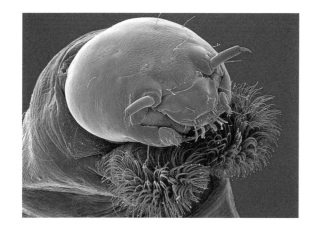

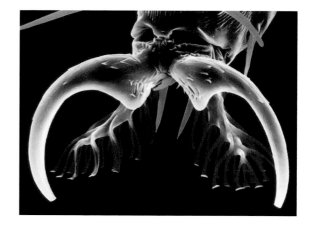
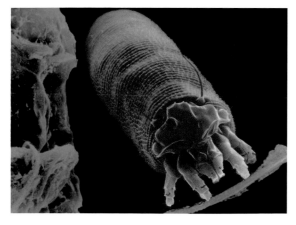

by Stephen Kramer

photographs by Dennis Kunkel

Houghton Mifflin Company

Boston 2001

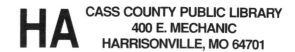

www.houghtonmifflinbooks.com

Book design by Lisa Diercks
The text of this book is set in Fairfield Light.

Library of Congress Cataloging-in-Publication Data
    Kramer, Stephen P.
    Hidden worlds : looking through a scientist's microscope / written by Stephen Kramer ; photographs by Dennis Kunkel.
        p. cm.—(Scientists in the field) Includes bibliographical references (p.).
    ISBN 0-618-05546-0
    1. Microscopy—Juvenile literature. 2. Microscopes—Juvenile literature. 3. Kunkel, Dennis—Juvenile literature. [1.
Microscopy. 2. Microscopes.] I. Kunkel, Dennis, ill. II. Title. III. Series.
    QH278 .K73 2001 570'.28'2—dc21 00-058083

Printed in Singapore
TWP 10 9 8 7 6 5 4 3 2 1

Photo Credits
Dennis Kunkel: pages 1, 2, 3, 6, 8, 9, 10, 11, 12, 13, 15, 17, 20, 21, 23, 25, 28 (left), 29, 31, 34, 36, 39, 41, 42, 44, 45, 50, 51, 54, 55, 56; Nancy Eckmann: pages 14, 16, 18, 24, 26, 27, 28 (right), 30, 33 (right), 37, 52; Stephen Kramer: pages 19, 35, 40, 43, 46, 47, 48, 49, 53; Charlene Tomas and Lara Kim Lee: page 22; Gordon Nishida: page 33 (left).

End leaf 1
Grainery weevil (SEM x50)

End leaf 2
Net-winged midge larva (SEM x65)

Page 1
top row, left to right:
Crazy ant head (SEM x40)
Radiolarian skeleton (SEM x375)
Tiger mosquito head (SEM x27)
bottom row, left to right:
Immature squid (SEM x16)
Leaf surface with trichome (SEM x100)
Spiny-backed spider (SEM x20)

Page 2
top row, left to right:
Saltwater copepod (SEM x15)
Diatom frustule (SEM x2,470)
Foraminiferan skeleton (SEM x245)
middle row, left to right:
Microbes on a kitchen cutting board
    (SEM x730)
Red blood cells in a capillary
    (SEM x2,680)
Neuron and astrocytic glial cell
    (SEM x2,120)
bottom row, left to right:
Jumping spider head (SEM x31)
Macrophage attacking *Escherichia coli*
    (SEM x2,730)
Damselfly head (SEM x13)

Page 3
top row, left to right:
Bloodworm head (SEM x520)
Small intestine villi (SEM x120)
Fruit fly tarsus and claw (SEM x1,290)
bottom row, left to right:
Leaf gall mite (SEM x570)
Leaf stomates (SEM x875)

To Jillian, Lei Lei, J. J., and Lydia
    —S. K.

*To my parents, Ed and Carmen Kunkel, for the Christmas gift
that started it all*
    —D. K.

Butterfly wing scales, the colorful, dustlike material that covers a butterfly's wings (SEM x900).

A Note to the Reader

Dennis Kunkel used microscopes to take many of the remarkable pictures in this book. Letters and numbers in parentheses in the captions describe the kind of microscope Dennis used and how many times the object is magnified. The letters DM mean the picture was taken with a dissecting microscope. CM means compound microscope. SEM stands for scanning electron microscope, and TEM stands for transmission electron microscope. The letter x is used to indicate magnification: x500 means that the object in the picture is 500 times its real size.

Since electron microscopes produce images that are only black and white, scientists sometimes use computers to color the images. Colors make it easier to see the shapes, textures, and structures in the pictures. The colors added in SEM and TEM pictures are not necessarily the natural colors you would see if you were looking at an object through a light microscope.

You may notice what resembles a backwards apostrophe in some Hawaiian words. This is not a punctuation mark but actually one of eight consonants in the Hawaiian language. Hawaiians call this glottal stop an 'okina. In the word Ko'olau it indicates a stop after the first syllable and gives each o an "oh" sound; thus, the word is pronounced "koh-oh-lau."

Imagine what it
would be like to . . .

look into the eyes of

a carpet beetle,

SEM x125

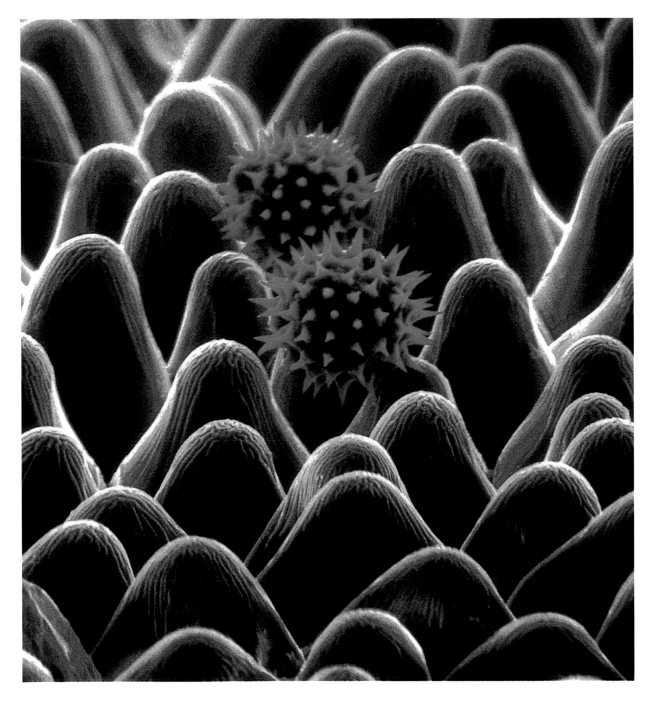

examine grains

of pollen on

a sunflower petal,

SEM x3,350

or take a peek at red blood cells the size of jelly doughnuts!

SEM x12,100

The fruiting stalks of a black mold (SEM x1,890). This kind of fungus can cause infections in humans.

There are hidden worlds in nature—places you can visit only with a microscope. If you know where and how to look, you will find beauty and surprises in the most unexpected places. Through the lenses of a microscope you can count the grains in a pinch of sand and see that each grain has a different size and shape. A microscope can make tiny, threadlike stalks of mold look like a bouquet of exotic flowers. And when

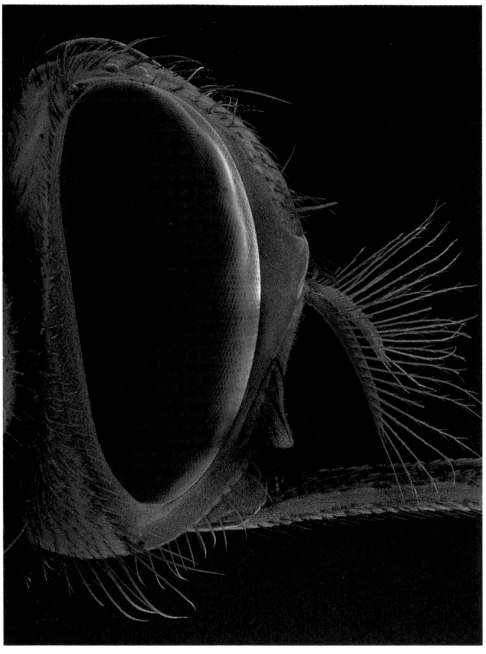

The head of a tsetse fly (SEM x48).

you observe a fly through a microscope, you may find it staring back at you with basketball-sized eyes!

Dennis Kunkel has spent most of his life exploring hidden worlds. He is a microscopist—a scientist who studies very small objects with a microscope. Dennis uses microscopes to look at things that most people don't even think about: a mosquito's foot, a single human hair, a sugar crystal, or the tiny scales on a butterfly's wing.

Scientists from all over the world ask Dennis for help. Like a detective, Dennis is never sure where his work will lead. He has examined pieces of meteorites to help astronomers learn what they are made of. This information is being used to answer questions about the beginning of our solar system. Dennis has worked with scientists who study ants. His ant pictures have helped them identify new species, learn about the different kinds of ant mouthparts, and understand how certain kinds of ants carry fungus to their underground nests. Dennis has even used microscopes to take pictures of spider silk secretion to help scientists figure out how the silk is produced and why it is so strong.

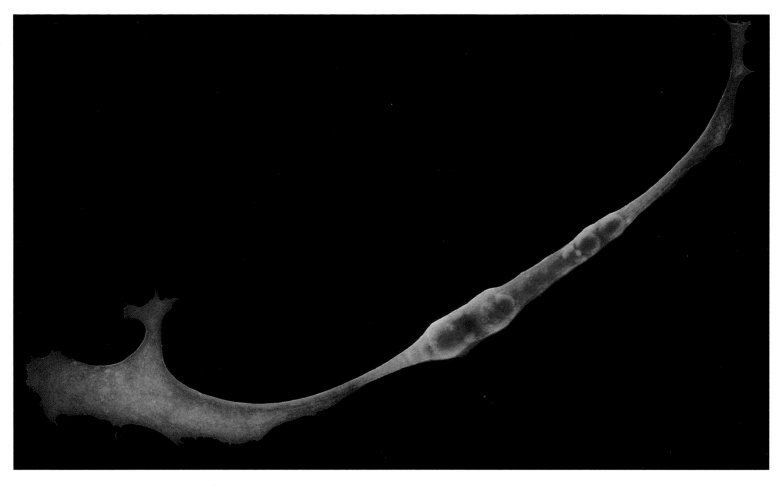

A cell from a smooth muscle, the type of muscle that moves food through your intestines (SEM x930).

Dennis has made scientific discoveries about bacteria, nerve and muscle cells, and very small organisms called protozoans. Much of his research has been published in scientific journals. But microscopes are more than just tools for answering scientific questions; they provide close-up views of some of nature's most interesting creatures and objects. The hidden worlds that Dennis Kunkel explores are remarkable places filled with curious and beautiful sights.

Becoming a Scientist

Dennis Kunkel grew up in the Iowa countryside, where cornfields stretched for miles in all directions. Dennis helped tend the flowers and vegetables in the family garden. He went on weekend fishing trips with his parents and his sisters, and he took care of the family pets. Dennis loved nature and being outdoors, but he did not know that someday he would become a scientist.

Then Dennis received a gift that changed his life. "When I was ten years old, my parents gave me a microscope for Christmas," he recalls. "It came with a set of prepared slides—things like insect legs, root hairs, and tiny creatures called protozoans. As soon as I unwrapped the microscope, I forgot about my other presents and tried to figure out how to use it."

The prepared specimens that came with the microscope were dead. Dennis quickly discovered that it was more fun to observe things that were alive and moving, so he began to take collecting trips. One of Dennis's first trips was to a pond about a mile and a half from his house. "I started hiking down there with my little collecting bottles and bringing back water samples to look at under my microscope," he explains. "I couldn't wait to get home from school in the afternoon so I could go to the pond. Before long I was looking at all kinds of fascinating creatures."

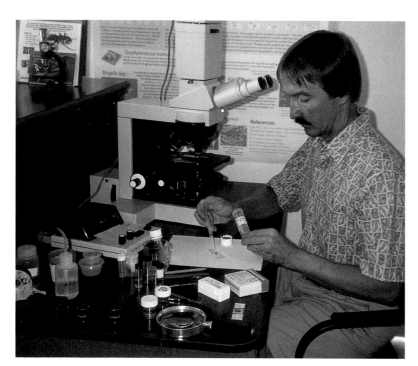

Dennis working at one of his microscopes. In the upper left-hand corner, you can see his first microscope.

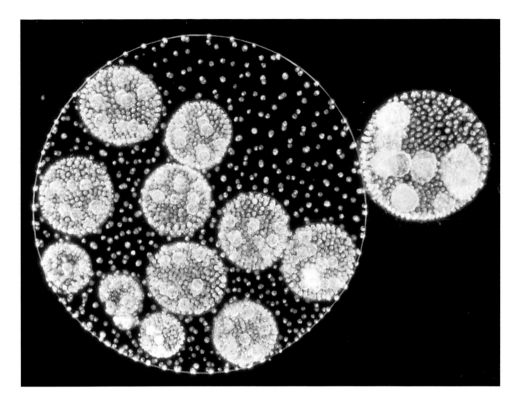

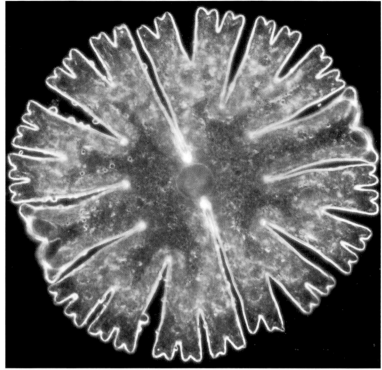

Dennis used his microscope to look at anything he could fit under its lenses. He examined insects, soil samples, and parts of plants. He looked at fur from his pets and seeds from nearby fields. Dennis made drawings of the things he observed, and he spent many hours reading about them.

After Dennis graduated from high school, he enrolled in a junior college in his hometown. A biology teacher there encouraged his love of science and microscopes. Dennis often worked in the science lab after school, using microscopes to study the things he collected.

Then Dennis transferred to the University of Washington, in Seattle. Finally he could learn and do things he had dreamed about. "I had the chance to work in labs with good

When Dennis looked at pond water with his first microscope, he saw these kinds of simple plants. They are green algae. *Left: Volvox* (CM x165). *Right: Micrasterias* (CM x335).

Dennis as a student, ready to dive.

microscopes," explains Dennis. "I spent hours speaking with professors and students about science. I had dreamed of exploring and learning about undersea life like Jacques Cousteau, but until I left Iowa I had never even seen the ocean. While I attended the University of Washington, I learned how to scuba dive. It was thrilling to go underwater to observe and collect the plants and animals I wanted to study."

In graduate school, Dennis began to use the science department's electron microscopes for his own research, studying tiny living things called cyanobacteria. But Dennis also used the microscopes to help other scientists. He helped one of his professors study and classify pollen grains from different kinds of flowers. He helped a fellow graduate student examine wood with an electron microscope to learn about how plant cells deposit minerals and create "hard" wood. He helped other students with their studies of algae, fungi, and flowering plants.

After eight years of graduate work—including thousands of hours of research and work with microscopes—Dennis earned a Ph.D. in botany, the study of plants. Although Dennis was finishing his schooling, he was just beginning a lifetime of scientific learning and discovery.

Dennis worked on research projects at the University of Washington and the University of Hawai'i for about twenty-five years. Now he does much of his work in his home on the island of O'ahu, Hawai'i.

Some people are allergic to pollen. Here are several types of pollen that cause watery eyes, runny noses, and sneezing: poplar (orange), alder (dark green), timothy grass (light green), ragweed (spiked yellow), sagebrush (oval yellow), and Scotch broom (plum) (SEM x1,600).

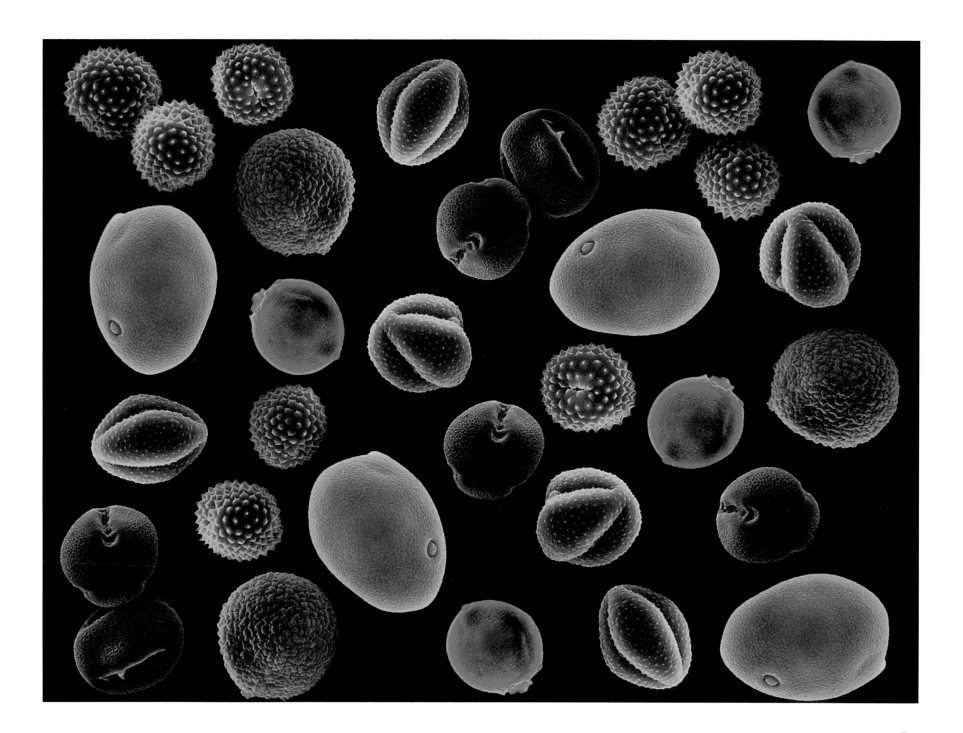

Working As a Scientist

Scientists are explorers. They usually make discoveries by asking questions and then trying to answer them. Some scientists find their answers in laboratories, surrounded by equipment and instruments. Others travel to natural areas to find their answers. Dennis's work has taken him to mountains, rainforests, deserts, caves, beaches, and into the sea.

Whenever Dennis goes on field trips, he takes along collecting boxes and bottles. When he returns to the lab, the boxes and bottles are usually full of interesting specimens: algae, lichens, mushrooms, seeds, leaves, insects, bark, soil, and flowers. Dennis has explored hidden worlds in places ranging from the blast zone of a volcano to the dust balls underneath people's beds!

Dennis examines the flower of a Brazilian oak near his home in Hawai'i.

Mount St. Helens

In 1980, a dormant volcano called Mount St. Helens erupted in Washington State. The blast from the eruption flattened huge forests of tall trees. Floods of boiling mud and water from melting snow scoured riverbeds. The countryside was covered with a thick layer of ash for miles around.

Some of the first people allowed to visit the blast zone were biologists, scientists who study living things. They were stunned by the destruction. One of the first things they wanted to know was whether any living things had survived.

A team of scientists from the University of Washington made plans to study the

An assortment of containers that Dennis uses for collecting specimens in the field.

lakes and streams in the blast area. Since Dennis was an expert on algae, the simple plants found in lakes and streams, he was invited to help with the study. The scientists traveled to a camp set up on the north side of Mount St. Helens. Twice a day, a helicopter flew them into the blast zone. All they could see, for miles in every direction, were dead trees blanketed by a heavy layer of ash.

The scientists were thrilled because they had never explored the area around an active volcano so soon after this type of eruption. But no one knew when the mountain might erupt again. In fact, no one even knew for sure whether it was safe to land a helicopter in the blast zone. Some pilots thought the ash stirred up by the whirling helicopter blades might choke the engines. So Dennis and the other scientists weren't

Dennis traveling to lakes in the volcano's blast zone.

Dennis and the scientific team collect water samples.

allowed to land in the study area on the first few trips. They had to collect their water samples while the helicopter was in the air!

As Dennis and the team crisscrossed the blast zone in the helicopter, they kept their eyes open for water. When they spotted a lake or pond that had survived the blast, the pilot flew the helicopter into position. As the helicopter hovered over the murky gray water, Dennis lowered collecting bottles on ropes. The bottles had triggers so Dennis could open them at different depths. This allowed him to collect some water samples from near the surface and others from deep in the lakes.

The first water samples the scientists collected showed that some of the lakes were completely dead. Nothing had survived the heat, gases, and choking ash of the eruption.

Just a few weeks later, Dennis used microscopes to look at new water samples he had collected from the same lakes. He was amazed to see algae, protozoans, and bacteria living in the water. Within several months, small crustaceans—animals that feed on algae and bacteria—began to reappear in some of the lakes.

Dennis and the other scientists kept careful records of the kinds of living things that returned to the lakes and

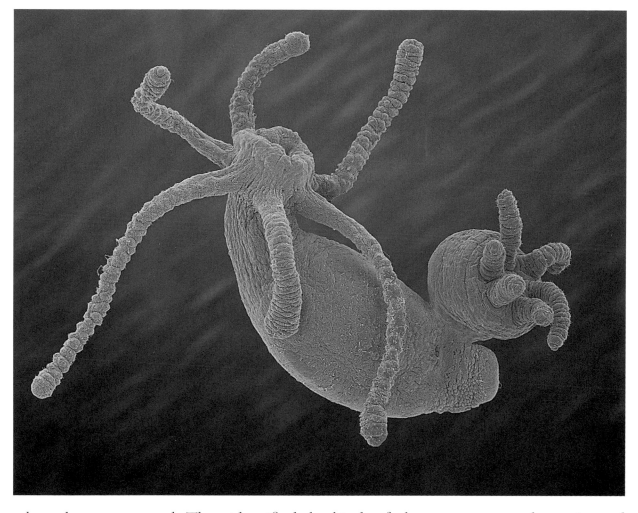

Hydra, a microscopic creature related to jellyfish, is one kind of life that Dennis found in the lakes and streams of the blast zone (SEM x84).

when they reappeared. They identified the kinds of algae, protozoans, bacteria, and crustaceans they found. Later, Dennis and the team also discovered that frogs and fish were returning to some of these lakes, apparently carried in by surrounding streams. Their studies helped other scientists understand what happens to life in lakes when a nearby volcano erupts—and how living things eventually return to areas where all life was destroyed.

Muscle cells

When Dennis worked at the University of Hawai'i, visitors to his laboratory sometimes found him holding a frog. Dennis spent six years doing research on South African clawed frogs to learn about muscle cells.

Muscle cells are different from other cells in your body because they can contract, or become shorter. When you decide to wiggle your finger, your brain sends a message through your nerves to the muscles that control your fingers. The nerve cells release a chemical that causes the muscle cells to contract. When muscles contract, they pull on the bones in your finger and make your finger move.

Being able to contract your muscles just the right amount and at the right time allows you to hold a pencil and write a letter or pick up a basketball and shoot it through a hoop. Many complex chemical and electrical signals have to happen at just the right time and in just the right place for your muscles to work.

Dennis is especially curious about how muscle cells develop the ability to interact with nerve cells—how they can pick up chemical messages from nerves that tell them to contract. He decided to study this development in embryos of South African clawed frogs. An embryo is a group of cells that develops from a fertilized egg and, in the case of a frog, grows into a tadpole.

By using microscopes, Dennis could identify which cells in the embryos would turn into muscle cells. As the cells

Dennis and a graduate student examine a South African clawed frog.

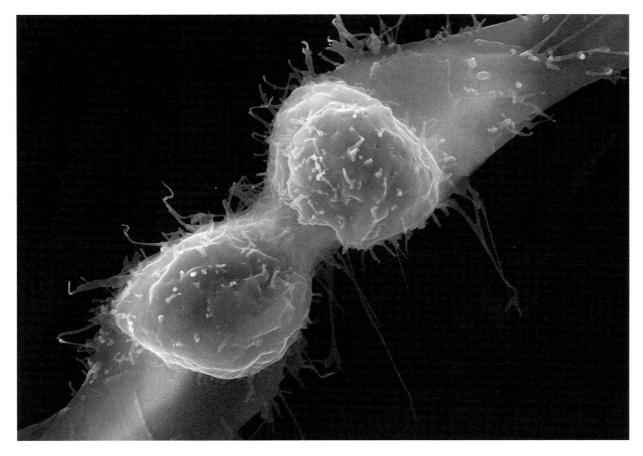

A myoblast, a type of embryo cell that grows and develops into a muscle cell (SEM x5,880). This myoblast is in the process of dividing.

developed and changed, he examined them with microscopes. Dennis spent much of his time studying muscle cell membranes, the "skin" that surrounds muscle cells. He also took many pictures of the cells with his microscopes.

These studies gave him a close-up look at how a growing muscle cell changes its membrane to allow a nerve cell to communicate with it. Dennis was able to watch simple embryo cells grow into specialized muscle cells that could receive messages from a nerve. The things Dennis learned about how a muscle cell develops may someday help doctors find better ways to treat people with muscle diseases.

Box jellyfish

If you walk along the beaches of O'ahu's south coast ten days after the full moon, you might find Dennis hiking along the shore or poking around in tide pools. He's looking for box jellyfish, a sea creature about as large as your hand. Much of its body is clear and jellylike, so it's very hard to see when it's swimming.

Box jellyfish live most of their lives deep in the ocean— perhaps as deep as 1,500 feet. But ten days after the full moon, they appear in shallow water near land. Some scientists think that they come to shallow water to reproduce. Sometimes the wind and waves bring them very close to the shore, or even onto the beach.

Several types of jellyfish can be found along Hawai'i's beaches. Here Dennis examines a type of jellyfish called the Portuguese man-of-war.

When box jellyfish appear near shore, lifeguards post signs warning swimmers to stay out of the water. Box jellyfish have tentacles that dangle below their bodies. The tentacles contain stinging cells called nematocysts. A nematocyst is like a tiny harpoon. If a swimming fish brushes against a tentacle, nematocysts "fire," injecting spiny threads containing venom into the fish's body. If the fish absorbs enough venom, it dies and the jellyfish consumes it. People who swim in the ocean sometimes get stung by the jellyfish as well.

Several years ago, a biologist was swimming in the surf near Waikiki Beach when she brushed against the tentacles of a box jellyfish. As she tried to get away, the tentacles became wrapped around her upper body. By the time she got to shore, the jelly-

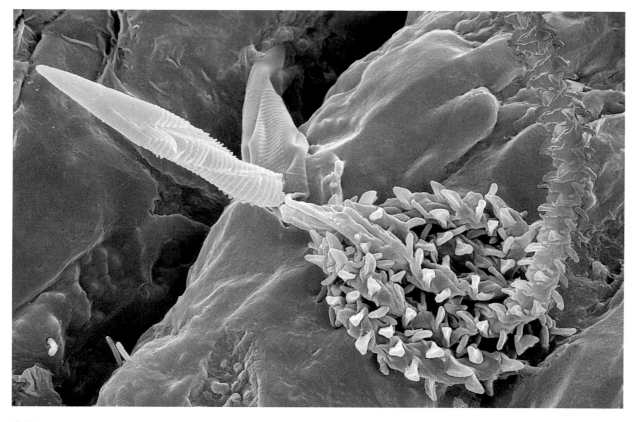

The harpoonlike structure and sharp spines of a box jellyfish tubule (SEM x3,530). *Specimen courtesy of Dr. Angel Yanagihara, University of Hawai'i, Honolulu.*

fish's nematocysts had injected so much venom into her that she had to be treated by paramedics.

Little is known about the box jellyfish and its venom. So, when the scientist recovered, she decided to study box jellyfish. Dennis heard about her research and thought it sounded interesting. He called and offered to use microscopes to study how a box jellyfish injects venom into its prey—or into people who brush against them while swimming.

The nematocyst of a box jellyfish is a capsule or sac that's shaped like a football. Inside the sac is a threadlike structure called a tubule that has many spines or sharp points.

When a box jellyfish's nematocyst fires, the tubule shoots out of the sac. Tubules are only about as long as the period at the end of this sentence, but they can puncture or tear soft tissue. Toxin from the nematocysts enters through the wound.

When Dennis examined box jellyfish nematocysts with microscopes, he noticed that their spines have a unique triangular shape. This discovery may help explain how box jellyfish can inject their venom into human skin so effectively. The nematocyst studies that Dennis is working on may someday be helpful in developing better treatments for swimmers who accidentally tangle with box jellyfish.

Studying unusual life

Dennis loves exploring Hawai'i's unusual environments and looking for interesting kinds of life. Hawai'i Volcanoes National Park, on the island of Hawai'i, has vents where poisonous gases and scalding steam blast out of the ground. Dennis has to be careful about poking his hands and head in at the edge of these vents, but he has discovered bacteria, mosses, and fungi living there.

Hawai'i has many lava tubes—caves formed when lava flowed underground from the mountains to the sea. The caves are homes to insects, spiders, and fungi that have adapted to life in the darkness underground. Sometimes Dennis explores these lava tubes, looking for specimens to collect.

Dennis also investigates the aquatic life in an unusual pond on the Kona coast, along the west side of the island of Hawai'i. One afternoon, Dennis and his wife, Nancy, were hiking through a lava field along trails made by wild donkeys. In the distance they saw palm trees growing in the rocks, so they headed over to investigate.

Dennis collecting moss, fungi, and sulfur crystals at the edge of some volcanic vents in Hawai'i Volcanoes National Park.

When they reached the trees, they were surprised to find a small pond.

Fish darted back and forth in the water, and insects hovered over the surface. The most beautiful thing about the pond, however, was its color. The rocks in the pond were covered with an unusual, golden brown plantlike material that made the water shimmer in the late-afternoon sunlight. Dennis and Nancy decided to call their discovery Golden Pond.

Dennis scraped some of the strange-colored material off the rocks and took it back to the lab to examine with his microscopes. He found that it was a filamentous bacterium—a kind of bacterium that grows in hairlike strands. Dennis also began searching for information about the pond. The pond is near the Kamehameha Trail, a path used by Hawaiians in ancient times. Because it was near the trail, it was probably used for drinking water.

Dennis has returned to the pond to study its algae, shrimplike amphipods, and other aquatic life. He's excited about monitoring the life in this pond for several reasons. First, the pond is the only source of fresh water in a large, dry lava field—so the aquatic creatures that live in it are very isolated. Second, the fresh water that enters the pond comes

Dennis collecting Pele's hair from a lava field. These delicate, hairlike strands of volcanic glass are formed when wind blows and stretches lava as it cools.

Left: The golden brown bacteria found in mats on the rocks of Golden Pond grow in twisting, threadlike strands (SEM x2,350).

Right: Dennis examines and collects the aquatic life in Golden Pond.

through lava tubes from distant mountains. And third, a mat of unusual filamentous bacteria covers the sides and bottom of the pond. By observing and keeping track of life in the pond over time, Dennis will learn how the creatures in this unusual little oasis adapt to one another and to changes in their environment.

Working with students

Dennis believes that it's important for scientists to help students develop an interest in science. One day, as Dennis was getting a haircut, he talked to the woman cutting his hair about his work as a microscopist. The woman mentioned that her daughter was looking for an idea for a science fair project, and Dennis volunteered to help. Dennis talked with the student about some research ideas, and they decided it might be interesting to compare the sand found on different Hawaiian beaches.

Dennis and the student collected sand from several beaches and examined the samples under a scanning electron microscope. They were able to tell which particles of

The aquatic nymph stage of the mayfly (SEM x31). Adult mayflies are slender flying insects found around streams and ponds.

sand came from rock and which came from coral or seashells. By the time they had finished studying the samples, they could even determine where an unknown sample of beach sand had come from, based on what it looked like under the microscope.

Dennis examines leaves with two young scientists.

Have you ever heard of dust mites? They are tiny creatures that live in carpets, feather pillows, and dust balls underneath beds. Dennis helped a group of high school students study them. The students used special brushes to comb rugs in their homes. They brought in dust balls from under beds and furniture. They looked at their samples with light and scanning electron microscopes.

It didn't take very long for the students to become dust mite experts. While they were examining and counting dust mites with microscopes, they discovered another, larger type of mite that preys on dust mites. The students also found that they could raise dust mites by putting them in a container with a dust ball and a bit of dry cat food.

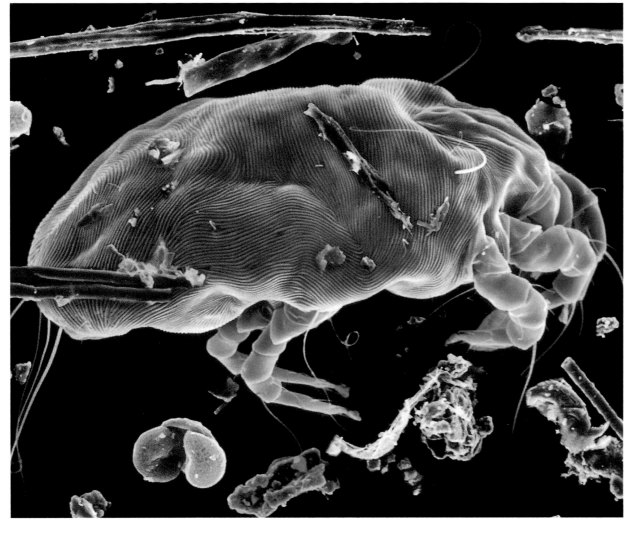

A dust mite surrounded by particles of dust (SEM x560). The dust in this picture includes cloth fibers, bits of skin, and pollen.

The students found the most dust mites in places where dust and cloth come into contact with human skin—such as bedding and pillowcases. The students also found that vacuum bags are likely to be crawling with dust mites. Many people are allergic to dust mite feces. So, if you find yourself sneezing when you change the bag in your vacuum cleaner, dust mites may be the problem.

Magnifying Mosquitoes

Like most people who spend time outdoors, Dennis has had plenty of experience with mosquitoes. When he goes hiking in Hawai'i's forests, he makes sure there's a bottle of mosquito repellent in his pack. But Dennis is also interested in mosquitoes as a scientist. Mosquitoes cause human health problems in many parts of the world because of diseases they carry, such as malaria and yellow fever. Scientists have used microscopes to learn about these diseases and about how mosquitoes transmit them to humans.

Dennis is also interested in mosquitoes because of their unusual appearance. An adult mosquito is almost entirely covered with scales, and male mosquitoes have antennae that look like giant hairbrushes. The pesky buzzing of a mosquito can be annoying when you're trying to fall asleep on a summer night. But looking at a mosquito through a microscope will give you a new appreciation of these remarkable flying insects.

The type of instrument Dennis uses to look at a mosquito depends on what part of the mosquito he wants to see and how closely he wants to examine it.

Loupe

A loupe is like a small magnifying glass. Jewelers often use loupes to examine gemstones and jewelry. When Dennis is exploring outdoors, he usually wears a loupe on a cord around his neck. When he sees something he wants to examine, he puts the loupe up to his eye. Looking at the object through a loupe makes it appear 5 times larger than its actual size.

This is a close-up view of an Asian tiger mosquito, as it might be seen through a loupe (x10). *Photograph courtesy of Gordon Nishida, Bishop Museum, Honolulu, Hawai'i.*

Dennis uses his loupe to examine a hibiscus flower.

A loupe is easy to use, easy to carry, and it gives Dennis a good first look at an object. Although a loupe doesn't magnify as much as a microscope, it can reveal many remarkable details about a mosquito.

Light Microscopes

Dissecting microscope. When Dennis wants to get a closer view of a mosquito, he uses a dissecting microscope. These microscopes are often used by scientists to dissect plants or animals. A dissecting microscope is like a powerful magnifying glass. It has glass lenses that make an object look about 10 times to 100 times larger than it really is.

Suppose, for example, that you put a single drop of pond water on a piece of white tile. If you look carefully at the drop, you might be able to see a tiny speck moving around in the water.

If you examine the drop of water with a dissecting microscope, you'll get a much better look at the speck. You might be able to see that the speck has eight legs. You might even be able to tell that the speck is a tiny creature called a water mite.

A dissecting microscope, like a loupe, is usually used for looking at the outside surface of objects. It can give you a close-up look at the hairs on a fly's leg, the surface of a leaf or flower, or the threads in a piece of cloth.

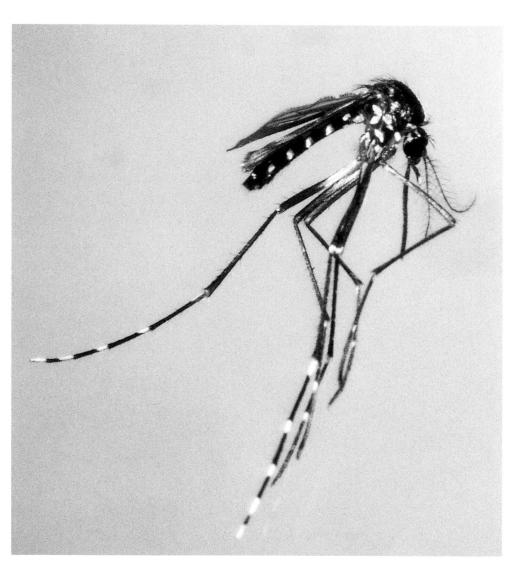

If you look at an Asian tiger mosquito through a dissecting microscope, this is what you'll see (DM x14).

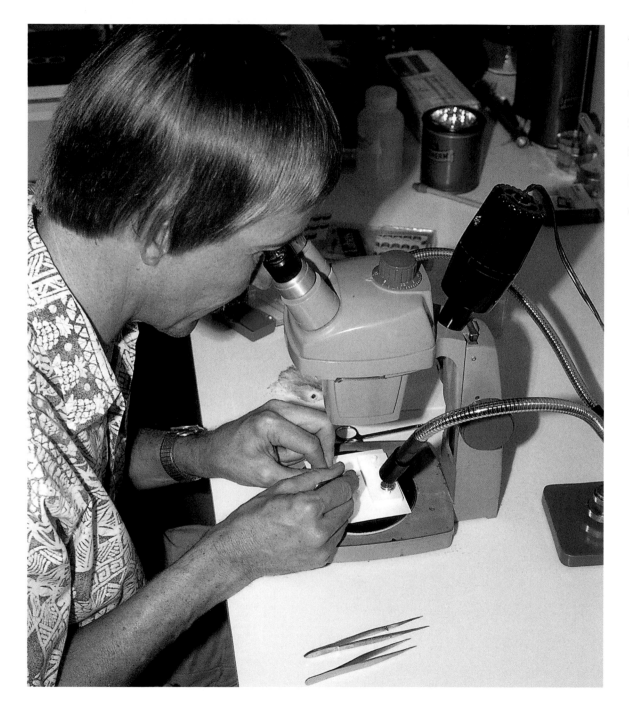

A dissecting microscope is the simplest type of microscope to use. To examine a dead mosquito, all Dennis needs to do is put it on a flat surface beneath the lenses. Then he shines a small light on the mosquito. Finally, he uses knobs on the microscope to bring the mosquito into focus.

Compound microscope. After Dennis has examined a mosquito with a dissecting microscope, he might decide to look at it with a compound microscope. Like dissecting microscopes, compound microscopes magnify objects with glass lenses. A compound microscope can make something look about 100 times to 1,500 times larger than it really is.

Compound microscopes are very useful for looking at cells, the tiny parts that living things are made of. The lenses of a compound microscope collect light that passes through cells or reflects off their edges. Before compound microscopes were invented about three hundred years ago, no one even knew that living things were made of cells. Many early discoveries about cells were made by scientists using compound microscopes.

Two views of an Asian tiger mosquito wing, seen through a compound microscope.

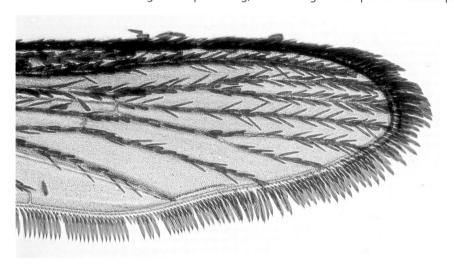

CM x75

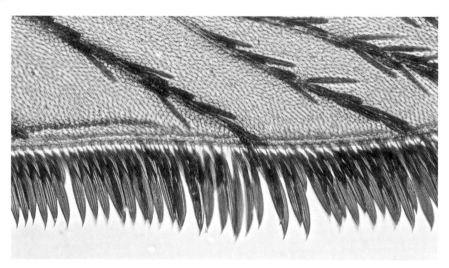

CM x190

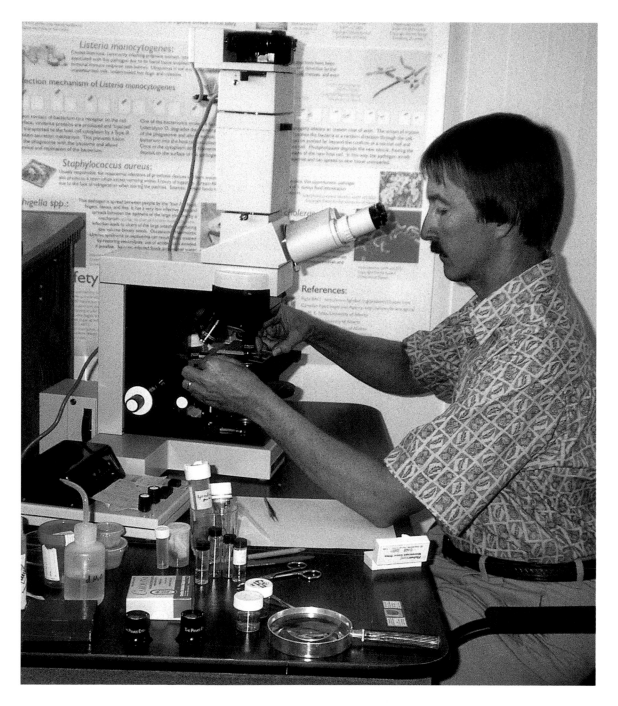

Using a compound microscope is more complicated than using a dissecting microscope. Dennis begins by using a small pair of tweezers to carefully lay a mosquito wing on a glass slide. Then he takes a very thin piece of glass called a coverslip and lays it over the wing. The coverslip flattens the wing and keeps it from moving around.

Moist specimens are often examined in a drop of water. The water keeps them from drying out and shriveling up. Since the mosquito wing is dry, Dennis decides not to add any water.

Finally, Dennis takes the glass slide and puts it on the stage, the flat surface beneath the lenses. Light shines from below the stage, up through the wing, and into the lenses of the microscope. Dennis adjusts the knobs to bring the mosquito wing into focus.

Dennis using a compound microscope.

Electron Microscopes

Scanning electron microscope. To look at a mosquito in even more detail, Dennis uses a scanning electron microscope. A scanning electron microscope, or SEM, magnifies objects from about 10 times to 300,000 times. The SEM is used to look at the surface of an object. It can provide much closer views and show more details than light microscopes.

The SEM doesn't use light to make images. The SEM image is created by using a beam of electrons and electromagnetic lenses. These lenses are tiny magnets that help collect and focus the beam of electrons. The electron beam allows the SEM to have much higher magnifications and show objects in more detail than light microscopes can.

The images produced by the SEM show up on a screen, but they have no color. They look like the pictures you would see on a black-and-white TV. To make the pictures more interesting and highlight important features, scientists sometimes add color.

Before coloring an SEM picture, Dennis prints a black-and-white copy. Then he lays a sheet of tracing paper on top of the picture. Dennis uses a pencil to outline the mosquito on the tracing paper. He traces the parts of the mosquito that he wants to highlight and writes numbers or letters inside the parts to show what color each should be. After Dennis has made decisions about the colors, the picture is colored using a computer program.

The pictures on the facing page show six views of an Asian tiger mosquito. The pictures were taken at different magnifications with the SEM, focusing on the wing.

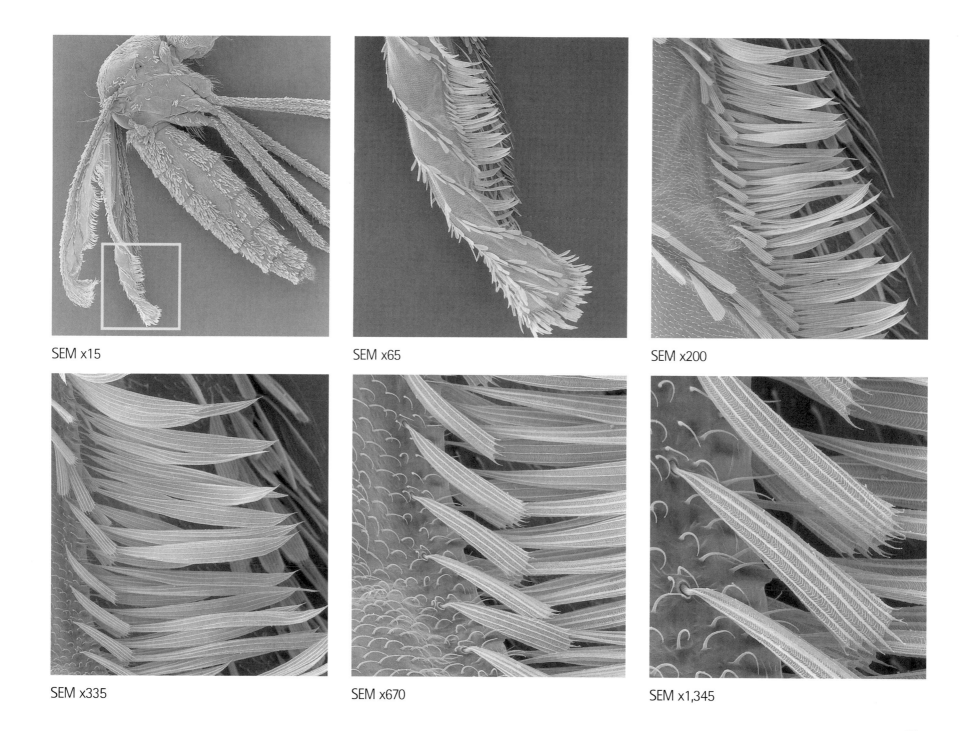

SEM x15

SEM x65

SEM x200

SEM x335

SEM x670

SEM x1,345

A specimen has to be carefully prepared before it can be examined with a scanning electron microscope. Dennis needs to dry his specimens completely before he can use them. If a moist specimen is placed in the SEM, water in the specimen will evaporate rapidly and may damage it.

Dennis lets the dead mosquito he wants to examine dry for two or three days. Then he uses double-sided tape to attach it to a piece of metal called a stub. Now Dennis can handle the stub without damaging the dried, fragile insect.

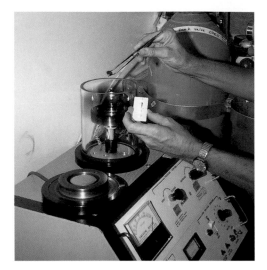

Placing the stub and specimen into the sputter coater.

Dennis places the stub, with the mosquito, into a piece of equipment called a sputter coater. The sputter coater coats the mosquito with a very thin layer of gold atoms. The surface layer of gold will allow the electron beam to create an image of the mosquito.

After Dennis removes the gold-coated mosquito from the sputter coater, he places the stub with the specimen into the chamber of the SEM. Then he switches on the vacuum pump. The vacuum pump pulls air out of the chamber so atoms and molecules in the air don't scatter the electron beam. Finally, he turns on the electron beam. The SEM uses electromagnetic lenses to focus the beam on the mosquito.

Electrons from the beam strike the gold-covered mosquito. As they do, the gold coating releases other electrons, which go flying off. These electrons are picked up by sensors in the microscope and sent to a viewing screen. By adjusting the knobs, Dennis can change the magnification, bring the mosquito into focus, and look at different parts of it. Dennis can also take a picture to make a record of what he sees.

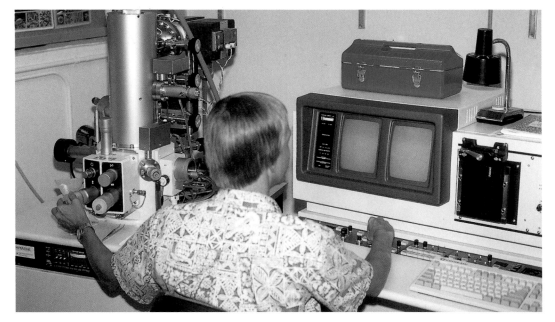

Examining the specimen with the scanning electron microscope.

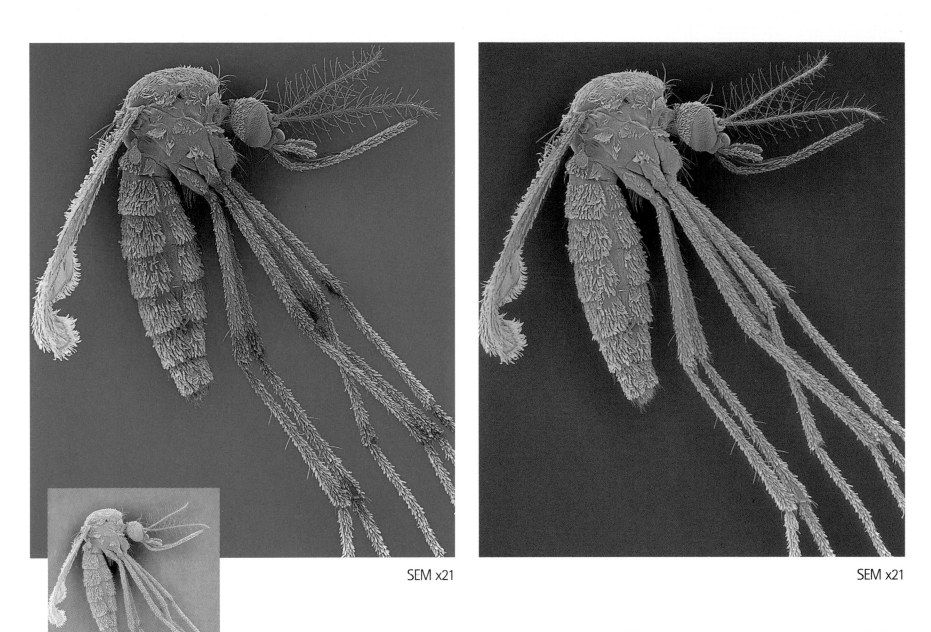

SEM x21

SEM x21

SEM x8

The original SEM picture of an Asian tiger mosquito and two different ways the picture was colored. Neither of the colored pictures shows the real color of a tiger mosquito, which is mostly dark gray with white stripes, but the colors used on these pictures make it much easier to see the details and parts of the mosquito.

Transmission electron microscope. If Dennis wants to look very closely at part of a mosquito, he can use a transmission electron microscope (TEM). Like the SEM, the TEM produces a picture by using an electron beam. It can magnify objects up to about 1,000,000 times.

The TEM is used to look through very thin sections of things. Scientists often use it to look inside cells. Dennis has used a TEM in his studies of cyanobacteria, nerve cells, and plant cells.

This TEM picture shows the nucleus, or control center, of a neuroglial cell from an Asian tiger mosquito (TEM x22,925). This kind of cell is a supporting cell that is found near mosquito nerve cells.

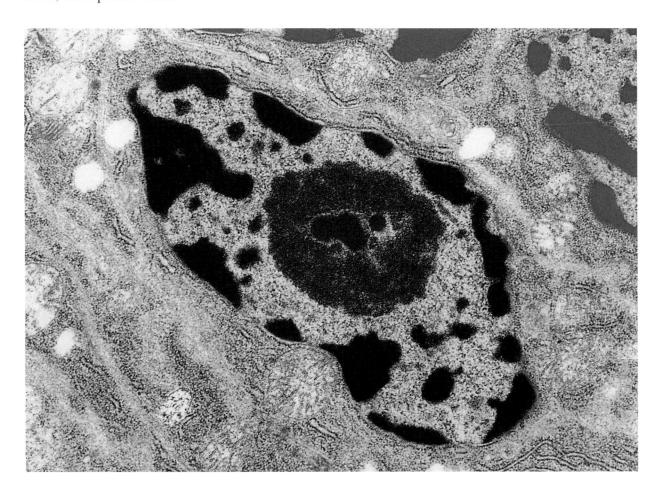

If Dennis wants to look at a mosquito neuroglial cell with the TEM, he has to cut a very thin slice of it. First he preserves the mosquito in a liquid called formaldehyde. Next he soaks it in alcohol. Then Dennis soaks the mosquito in liquid resin, which enters the mosquito's body. When the resin is dried in an oven, it forms a clear, hard material in and around the mosquito.

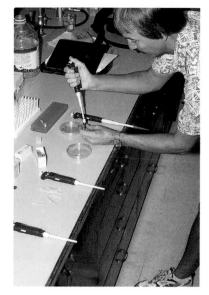

Preserving a mosquito.

Dennis uses an instrument called an ultramicrotome to cut thin slices through the resin that contains the mosquito. Four millionths of an inch is about the right thickness! Then he places the thin slices on a tiny metal grid of fine screen. Finally, he places the grid into a chamber in the TEM and turns on the vacuum pump.

After the air is removed from the TEM, Dennis turns on the electron beam and checks the picture on the screen, using control switches to make adjustments. Now he can look inside a neuroglial cell to see the parts that make it work, such as its nucleus, DNA, and proteins.

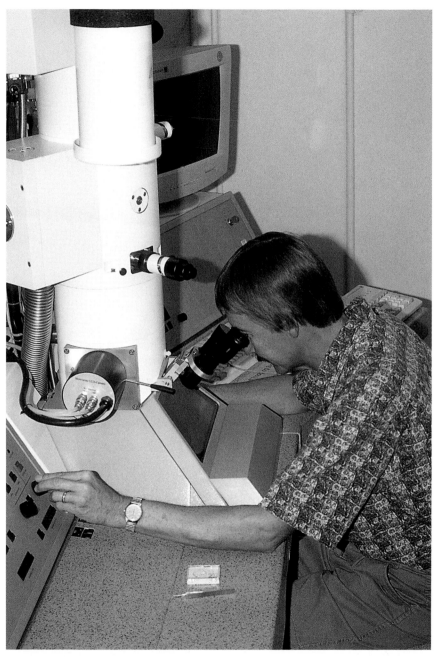

Using a transmission electron microscope.

Seeing Hidden Worlds in Nature

Dennis is always on the lookout for interesting specimens to examine. His wife, Nancy, shares his excitement in finding and learning about interesting new subjects. "Being around Dennis calls for a sense of humor and a tolerance for small creatures," she says.

Dennis was getting ready to plant some seeds in his garden when he noticed this bean weevil emerging from a seed (SEM x52).

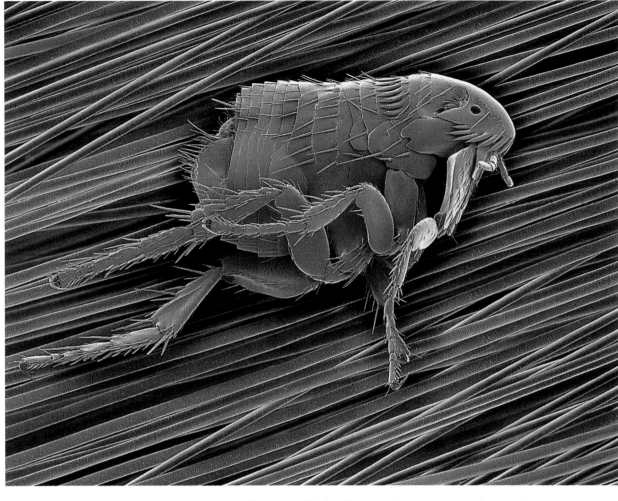

Dog flea on dog hair (SEM x42).
The powerful legs are used for jumping.

"Since we never know when or where we'll find something to study, we're sometimes without a box or bottle to put things in. There have been many times when Dennis has used my lipstick cap as a temporary home for an insect, a millipede, or a small spider."

Nancy is also a scientist. Together, she and Dennis keep their eyes peeled for interesting things, even in their house and out in their garden. Once they collected fleas to study from a stray dog who made a bed of one of their deck chairs!

Dennis checking his gear.

A scientist who studies birds often sees and hears birds that other people never even notice. A scientist who studies plants will observe things about trees and flowers that other people miss. Years of looking through microscopes has given Dennis a good sense of where to look for the curious and beautiful hidden worlds of nature. He sees things that most people walk right past. One of the best ways to learn how to see the hidden worlds of nature is to take a hike with Dennis.

When Dennis arrives at the trailhead, afternoon shadows are already creeping across the forest floor. He glances up at the sky to check the weather. Then he straps on his pack. It holds everything he'll need for his hike: water, sunscreen, insect repellent, a rain poncho, snacks, and collecting bottles.

The trail is muddy, and the forest has the fresh smell of soil and plants that have been washed by a tropical rain shower. But now the sun is out, and there are patches of blue sky overhead. In the distance, white clouds skitter up the steep slopes of Oʻahu's Koʻolau Mountains, pushed by trade winds that blow off the Pacific Ocean.

As he walks through the forest, Dennis glances up at the branches of the monkey pod, banyan, paperbark, candle-nut, and ironwood trees that stretch high overhead. But Dennis spends much of his time looking at leaves, bark, and flowers near the ground.

A short distance up the trail, he suddenly stops.

"Do you smell that?" he asks. "There's a tree dropping fruit nearby."

Dennis scans the uphill side of the trail and pulls back the branches of a large bush. There, scattered on the ground beneath a tree, are the ripe and decaying fruits of a wild mango tree. Dennis smiles.

"See those tiny insects hovering over the fruit?" he asks. "They're pomace flies."

Dennis slowly approaches one of the fallen mangoes, trying not to disturb the small flies. Crouching down, Dennis reaches for his loupe and peers through it at the flies and the larvae wriggling in the rotting fruit.

A moment later, he pulls a small plastic collecting jar out of his backpack. "I've examined these flies before," he says. "But I'm going to take a few back to the lab for another look."

With a quick swoop of Dennis's hand, the jar flashes through the air. While the container is still moving, he snaps the lid on and traps a couple of flies inside. Dennis tucks the specimens carefully in his pack.

Dennis capturing a specimen.

As he moves up the trail, the large white flowers of a wild ginger plant catch his eye. Dennis approaches and gently pulls the flower stalk closer. Holding the loupe to

The Ko'olau Mountains.

his eye, he examines the flower through the lens. With the loupe, he can see the shapes of even the smallest parts of the flower. Dustlike grains of pollen look like piles of golden baseballs. Tiny dots of yellow pigment on white petals are like dabs of paint on an artist's palette.

The trail winds up into a clearing on a hilltop ridge, and the peaks of the Koʻolau Mountains come into sight. The view is breathtaking. Ragged gray clouds cling to the sides of mountains that rise straight into the air.

Suddenly Dennis's attention shifts to a plant beside the trail. He kneels beside it, looking at the tiny hairs arranged in an intricate pattern along the edge of a single leaf of tall grass.

Examining a tropical grass plant.

Dennis moves the blade of grass slowly back and forth under his loupe, marveling at the amazing arrangement of its hairs. During the past few weeks, dozens of people have walked along this path. Many of them paused, at least for a moment, to look at the rugged, beautiful mountains stretching across the horizon. But most of the hikers walked right past this plant.

Dennis removes scissors from his pack and carefully snips a small blade of grass. He can almost visualize the picture he'll see when he puts the grass in the scanning electron microscope. There's work to do first, of course. The sample will have to be dried, mounted, and sputter coated with gold. It might take an hour of searching with the microscope to find just the right view of the grass, the one that best shows the graceful curve of the blade and the delicate hairs that cover it. And then color will be added to the picture, making some of the details easier to see.

But when the work is done, Dennis will have learned something new about the

Tiny spines and a delicate hair on the surface of a blade of grass (SEM x825).

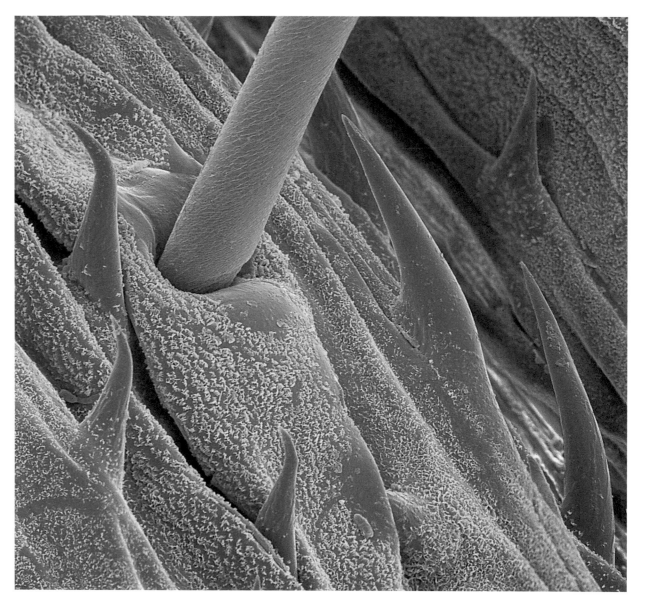

complex structure of a blade of grass. He will also have another work of art to add to his collection of photographs: a glimpse of the hidden world he discovered one rainy afternoon on a trail at the edge of the Koʻolau Mountains.

Sharing Hidden Worlds

○ ○ ○

Dennis is always looking for ways to share his glimpses of hidden worlds. "The most exciting thing about being a microscopist," says Dennis, "is being able to see new and interesting things. But another important thing, for me, is sharing this beauty with others. I especially enjoy sharing my pictures with young people."

Photographs of Dennis's microscopic images have been published in magazines such as *Time, Smithsonian, Discover, Scientific American,* and *National Geographic.* You can also find his pictures in newspapers, books, and calendars. A few poster-sized prints of his work were even used in the movie *Outbreak.*

Dennis also has a Web site for people who are curious about microscopic life. The Web site has many of Dennis's SEM and TEM images. If you'd like to visit Dennis's site, you can find it at www.DennisKunkel.com.

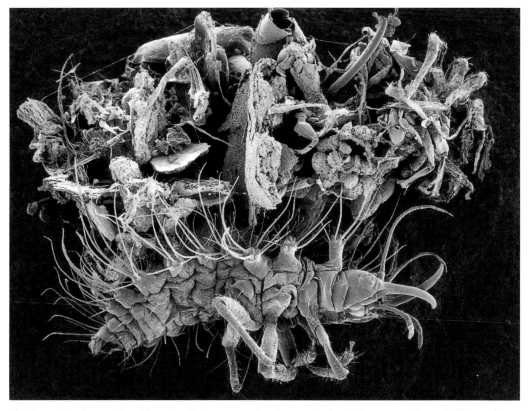

The lacewing larva piles bits of soil, leaves, and twigs on its back for camouflage (SEM x29).

How to Become a Scientist

Here is Dennis's advice for students who think they might like to become scientists:

Become an observer. One of the most important things you can do to become a good scientist and microscopist is practice being a careful observer. Find a comfortable chair and put it in the middle of your garden, yard, or a park. Sit in the chair for ten minutes or thirty minutes or an hour. Watch the insects that fly past or land on the plants. Look at the shapes of leaves and stems and branches. Listen to the sounds of buzzing bees and chirping crickets. See if you can find a sight or smell or sound that surprises you. Use a loupe or magnifying glass to look closely at interesting objects.

Learn everything you can about a topic that interests you. Suppose you'd like to explore flowers by using a microscope. Go to the library and check out some flower books. See what you can find on the Internet. Pick some flowers and carefully take them apart. Use a loupe or a magnifying glass to see how everything fits together. The more you know about flowers from reading about them and observing them, the more you'll understand when you begin looking at them with a loupe or a microscope.

Ask for help from a knowledgeable person. After you've learned everything you can on your own, ask someone else to help with questions you still have. Maybe there's someone at a nearby school or museum who knows about insects, spiders, algae, moss, or something else you'd like to learn about. If you don't have a microscope of your own, maybe a teacher would help you look at some specimens with a school microscope.

Find a scientist to talk to or find a place where scientific research is being done. If you

Dennis collecting at a pond.

Dennis looking closely at a fern leaf.

still want to learn more, you may be able to find a scientist to talk to at a nearby college, university, or research station. Write a letter or an e-mail message to the scientist, explaining what you're interested in. Ask if you can schedule a time to visit. Most scientists are happy to talk to students who share their passion for science.

Further Reading

The skeletons of saltwater diatoms, microscopic plants that live in the ocean (SEM x2,345).

Cobb, Vicki. *Blood and Gore*. New York: Scholastic, 1998.

———. *Dirt and Grime*. New York: Scholastic, 1998.

Levine, Shar, and Leslie Johnstone. *Fun with Your Microscope*. New York: Sterling Publishing Co., 1998.

———. *The Microscope Book*. New York: Sterling Publishing Co., 1996.

Rainis, Kenneth G., and Bruce J. Russell. *Guide to Microlife*. Danbury, Conn.: Franklin Watts, 1997.

Stewart, Gail B. *Microscopes: Bringing the Unseen World into Focus*. San Diego: Lucent Books, 1992.

Tomb, Howard, and Dennis Kunkel. *Microaliens: Dazzling Journeys with an Electron Microscope*. New York: Farrar, Straus & Giroux, 1993.

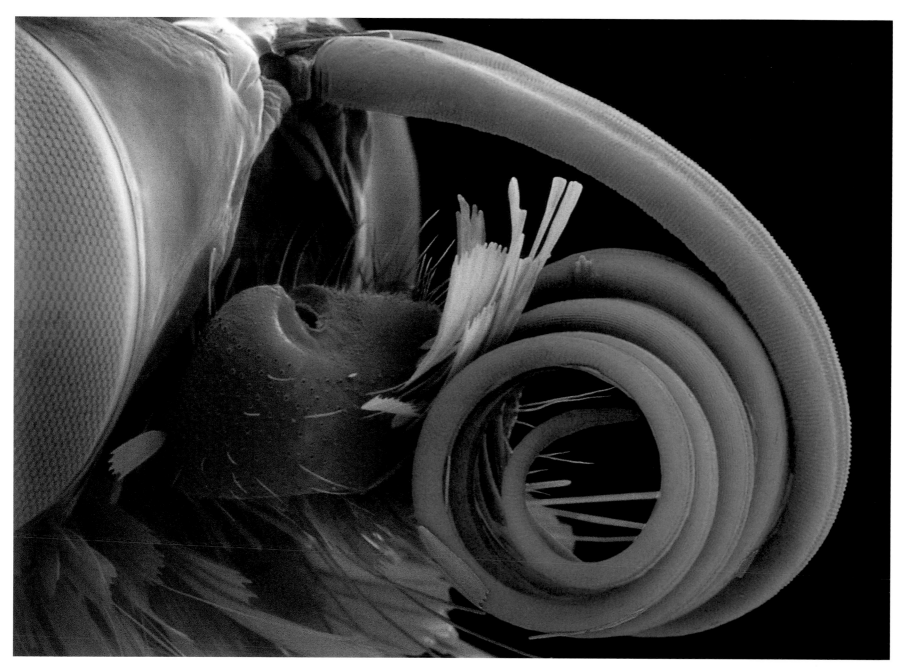

A butterfly's proboscis, the coiled mouthpart it uses to sip nectar (SEM x135).

Acknowledgments

○ ○ ○

Many people have made important contributions to this book. My son, Josh, suggested the idea of a book when he discovered Dennis Kunkel's remarkable images on the Web and insisted, "Dad, you've got to take a look at these pictures!"

I'm grateful to Dennis Kunkel for sharing his excitement about his work and for his patience in explaining microscopy to me, especially when I didn't "get it" the first time! The warm hospitality of Dennis and his wife, Nancy, during our visit to Kailua has left my wife and me with fond memories of delicious meals, beautiful botanical gardens, and delightful hikes through Hawai'i's tropical forests.

Two other scientists contributed to the book's images. The jellyfish nematocyst tubule was made from a specimen provided by Dr. Angel Yanagihara, PBRC, University of Hawai'i, Honolulu. The picture of the tiger mosquito is courtesy of Gordon Nishida, Bishop Museum, Honolulu.

Darcy Hu, of Hawai'i Volcanoes National Park, assisted Dennis with obtaining his permit to collect at the park. Thanks to Marilyn Dunlap, Ph.D. and Tina Weatherby Carvalho at the University of Hawai'i Biological EM Facility for their support. In addition, special thanks to Chris Porter Illustration for colorization of Dennis's SEM and TEM images. Finally, Dennis and I thank Amy Flynn, whose guidance, constructive ideas, and thoughtful editing were so important in helping this book take shape.

Vorticella, a single-celled protozoan (x1,495).

Index

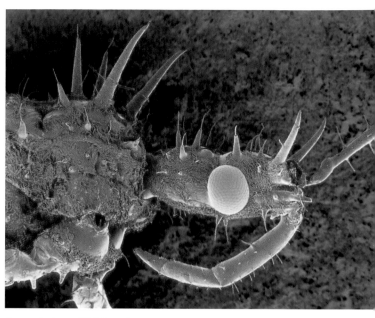

Assassin bug (SEM x21).